The Believer's Authority

Kenneth E. Hagin

Unless otherwise indicated, all Scripture quotations in this volume are from the *King James Version* of the Bible.

Second Edition
Twenty-Fourth Printing 1997

ISBN 0-89276-406-6

In the U.S. write:
Kenneth Hagin Ministries
P.O. Box 50126
Tulsa, OK 74150-0126

In Canada write:
Kenneth Hagin Ministries
P.O. Box 335, Station D,
Etobicoke (Toronto), Ontario
Canada, M9A 4X3

The Triumphant Church: Dominion Over All the Powers of Darkness
Healing Scriptures
Mountain-Moving Faith
Love: The Way to Victory
Biblical Keys to Financial Prosperity
The Price Is Not Greater Than God's Grace (Mrs. Oretha Hagin)

MINIBOOKS (A partial listing)

* *The New Birth*
* *Why Tongues?*
* *In Him*
* *God's Medicine*
* *You Can Have What You Say*
* *Don't Blame God*
* *Words*
Plead Your Case
* *How To Keep Your Healing*
The Bible Way To Receive the Holy Spirit .
I Went to Hell
How To Walk in Love
The Precious Blood of Jesus
* *Love Never Fails*
How God Taught Me About Prosperity

BOOKS BY KENNETH HAGIN JR.

* *Man's Impossibility — God's Possibility*
Because of Jesus
How To Make the Dream God Gave You Come True
The Life of Obedience
Forget Not!
God's Irresistible Word
Healing: Forever Settled
Don't Quit! Your Faith Will See You Through
The Untapped Power in Praise
Listen to Your Heart
What Comes After Faith?
Speak to Your Mountain!
Come Out of the Valley!
It's Your Move!
God's Victory Plan
Another Look at Faith

MINIBOOKS (A partial listing)

* *Faith Worketh by Love*
* *Seven Hindrances to Healing*
* *The Past Tense of God's Word*
Faith Takes Back What the Devil's Stolen
How To Be a Success in Life
Get Acquainted With God
Unforgiveness
Ministering to the Brokenhearted

---

*These titles are also available in Spanish. Information about other foreign translations of several of the above titles (i.e., Finnish, French, German, Indonesian, Polish, Russian, etc.) may be obtained by writing to: Kenneth Hagin Ministries, P.O. Box 50126, Tulsa, Oklahoma 74150-0126.

Contents

Preface

Foreword

Preface

My Dad wrote this book back in 1967. During the years, the important Bible truths in its pages have literally transformed the lives of many people.

Since 1967, however, Dad has gained even more light on the subject of spiritual authority. He often has said he wished this book could contain these further insights.

In 1984, in honor of Dad's 50th anniversary in the ministry, we reedited this book and added the information he always has wanted included. We are delighted to share this new, expanded book with you, our loyal partners and friends.

Kenneth Hagin Jr.

Foreword

Back in the 1940s, I asked myself the question, "Do we have authority that we don't know about — that we haven't discovered — that we're not using?"

I had had little glimpses of spiritual authority once in a while. Like others, I had stumbled upon it and had exercised it without knowing what I was doing. I wondered, "Is the Spirit of God trying to show me something?" So I began to study along this line, think along this line, feed along this line — and I began to see more and more light.

An article in *The Pentecostal Evangel* prompted my study on the words "power" and "authority." Then I came across a wonderful pamphlet entitled *The Authority of the Believer* by John A. MacMillan, a missionary to China who later edited *The Alliance Weekly*. (His pamphlet was reissued several years ago and is available from Christian Publications, Camp Hill, Pennsylvania.)

As a result of my studies, I concluded that we as a Church have authority on the earth that we've never yet realized — authority that we're not using.

A few of us have barely gotten to the edge of that authority, but before Jesus comes again, there's going to be a whole company of believers who will rise up with the authority that is theirs. They will know what is theirs, and they will do the work that God intended they should do.

Kenneth E. Hagin

Chapter 1
The Prayers of Paul

The authority of the believer is unveiled more fully in the Book of Ephesians than any other epistle written to the churches. Because this book is based on Ephesians, let me encourage you to read the first three chapters over and over again for several days.

You will notice there are Spirit-anointed prayers at the end of the first and third chapters. However, Paul didn't pray these prayers only for the Church at Ephesus. These prayers apply to us today just as much as they did to the believers at Ephesus, because they were given by the Holy Spirit.

EPHESIANS 1:16-20
16 [I] Cease not to give thanks for you, making mention of you in my prayers,
17 That the God of our Lord Jesus Christ, the Father of glory, may give unto you the spirit of wisdom and revelation in the knowledge of him:
18 The eyes of your understanding being enlightened; that ye may know what is the hope of his calling, and what the riches of the glory of his inheritance in the saints,
19 And what is the exceeding greatness of his power to usward who believe, according to the working of his mighty power,
20 Which he wrought in Christ, when he raised him from the dead, and set him at his own right hand in the heavenly places . . . .

EPHESIANS 3:14-19
14 For this cause I bow my knees unto the Father of our Lord Jesus Christ,
15 Of whom the whole family in heaven and earth is named,

16 That he would grant you, according to the riches of his glory, to be strengthened with might by his Spirit in the inner man;
17 That Christ may dwell in your hearts by faith; that ye, being rooted and grounded in love,
18 May be able to comprehend with all saints what is the breadth, and length, and depth, and height;
19 And to know the love of Christ, which passeth knowledge, that ye might be filled with all the fulness of God.

The turning point in my life came when I prayed these prayers for myself more than a thousand times. I started by reading them aloud, beginning with the first chapter. I personalized the prayers by saying "me" wherever Paul said "you."

For example, reading Ephesians 3:14-17, I would say, "For this cause *I* bow my knees unto the Father of *my* Lord Jesus Christ, Of whom the whole family in heaven and earth is named, That he would grant *me*, according to the riches of his glory, to be strengthened with might by his Spirit in the inner man; That Christ may dwell in *my* heart by faith . . . ."

I spent much time praying these two prayers on my knees at the altar of the last church I pastored in East Texas. I kept my Bible open before me to these prayers and prayed them for myself several times a day. Sometimes I told my wife I was going next door to the church to pray and didn't want to be bothered except in an emergency. Sometimes I stayed in prayer two or three days at a time.

I spent about six months praying this way during the winter of 1947-48. Then the first thing I was praying for started to happen. I had been praying for "the spirit of wisdom and revelation" (Eph. 1:17), and the spirit of revelation began to function! I began to see things in the Bible I had never seen before. It just began to open up to me.

I advanced more in spiritual growth and knowledge of the Word in those six months than I had in 14 years as a minister and in more than 16 years as a Christian.

That was one of the greatest spiritual discoveries I ever made.

I said to my wife, "What in the world have I been preaching? I was so ignorant of the Bible, it's a wonder the deacons didn't have to come by and tell me to get in out of the rain!"

We must have this spirit of wisdom and revelation of Christ and His Word if we are to grow. It is not going to be imparted to us through our intellect, either. The Holy Spirit must unveil it to us.

People often want to know how to pray for fellow Christians. If you start praying these Ephesian prayers for them, you'll see results in their lives. I suggest you pray the prayers for yourself, too.

Years ago, I prayed these prayers twice a day, morning and evening, for a family member. He needed healing desperately, yet he couldn't seem to grasp what the Bible teaches about divine healing.

When I prayed, I inserted this person's name in the prayers as I had previously inserted my own. Within 10 days, he wrote me, saying, "I'm beginning to see things I never saw before." (The minute you get scriptural, things happen.)

It was surprising how fast my kinfolks changed once I started praying for them scripturally. (I had been praying for some of them for years with no results.)

The Authority of the Believer

EPHESIANS 6:12
12 For we wrestle not against flesh and blood, but against principalities, against powers, against the rulers of the darkness of this world, against spiritual wickedness in high places.

Thank God we have authority over such evil spirits through Jesus Christ. We need to understand what Paul said here in the light of what he wrote in previous chapters. We need to realize that we have authority through Christ. *Our combat with the devil always should be with the consciousness that we have authority over him* because he is a defeated foe — the Lord Jesus Christ defeated him for us.

However, the authority of the believer is an aspect of the Christian walk that few believers know much about. Some think that authority over the devil belongs to only a few chosen people to whom God has given special power. It doesn't; it belongs to all the children of God!

We receive this authority when we are born again. *As we are made new creatures in Christ Jesus, we inherit the Name of the Lord Jesus Christ, and we can use it in prayer against the enemy.*

But the devil doesn't want Christians to learn about the authority of the believer. He wants to continue to defeat us anytime he wants. That's why he will do everything he can to keep Christians from learning the truth about authority; he will fight us more on this subject than anything else. He knows that when we learn the truth, his heyday will be over. We will dominate him, enjoying the authority that is rightfully ours.

Ephesians 1:3 reads, *"Blessed be the God and Father*

of our Lord Jesus Christ, who hath blessed us [the whole Church] *with all spiritual blessings in heavenly places in Christ.*" *The American Standard Version* renders "*all spiritual blessings*" as "*every spiritual blessing.*" This means every spiritual blessing there is. In Christ, all spiritual blessings belong to us. *Authority belongs to us whether we realize it or not.* But just knowing this isn't enough. It's knowledge acted upon that brings results! It's a tragedy for Christians to go through life and never find out what belongs to them.

Did you ever stop to think about it: Salvation belongs to the sinner. Jesus already has bought the salvation of the worst sinner, just as He did for us. That's the reason He told us to go tell the Good News; go tell sinners they're reconciled to God.

But we've never really told them that. We've told them God's mad at them and is counting up everything they've done wrong. Yet the Bible says God isn't holding anything against the sinner! God says He has cancelled it out.

That's what's so awful: The poor sinner, not knowing this, will have to go to hell even though all of his debts are cancelled! Second Corinthians 5:19 will tell you that.

There's no sin problem. Jesus settled that. There's just a sinner problem. Get the sinner to Jesus, and that cures the problem. Yes, that's a little different from what people have been taught, but it's what the Bible says.

The sinner doesn't know what belongs to him, so it won't do him any good. By the same token, if Christians don't know the things that belong to them, they won't do them any good. They need to find out about what belongs to them. That's why God put teachers in the Church. That's why God gave us His Word: to tell us what's ours.

In the natural world, too, things can be ours, yet if we don't know about them, they won't do us any good.

I've told about the time I hid a $20 bill in my billfold and forgot about it. Then I ran out of gasoline one day, started searching through my billfold, and found the $20 bill. I couldn't say I didn't have it, because I had it all the time — I had carried it around for months right in my hip pocket. Because I didn't know what I had, I couldn't spend it, but it was just as much mine when I didn't know about it as it was when I did.

Years ago I read about a man who was found dead in the small, shabby room he rented for $3 a week. He had been a familiar sight on the streets of Chicago for about 20 years, always dressed in rags and eating out of garbage cans.

When he wasn't seen for two or three days, concerned neighbors went to look for him and found him dead in bed. An autopsy revealed that he had died of malnutrition, yet a money belt found around his waist contained more than $23,000.

That man had lived in abject poverty, peddling newspapers for a living, yet he had money. He could have lived in the finest hotel in town instead of that little, run-down room. He could have eaten the best food instead of garbage. But he didn't use what belonged to him.

We need to know what belongs to us. Jesus said, *"And ye shall know the truth, and the truth shall make you free"* (John 8:32). In Hosea God says, *"My people* [not sinners, not the world] *are destroyed for lack of knowledge...."* (Hosea 4:6). People actually perish who wouldn't have to.

Chapter 2
What Is Authority?

The translators of the *King James Version* translated many words consistently, but not the Greek words for "power" and "authority."

For example, in the *King James Version*, Jesus says in Luke 10:19, *"Behold, I give unto you POWER to tread on serpents and scorpions, and over all the POWER of the enemy: and nothing shall by any means hurt you."*

Although the word "power" is used twice in this verse, two different words are found in the original Greek. What Jesus actually said was, "I have given you AUTHORITY to tread on serpents and scorpions, and over all the POWER of the enemy . . . ."

In speaking about "serpents and scorpions," Jesus is talking about the power of the devil — demons, evil spirits, and all his cohorts. We need to realize that we've got authority over them!

Does the Church of the Lord Jesus Christ have (or need) any less authority today than it had in the first century? It would be preposterous to think so, wouldn't it?

The value of our authority rests on the power that is behind that authority. *God Himself is the power behind our authority! The devil and his forces are obliged to recognize our authority!*

The believer who thoroughly understands that the power of God is backing him can exercise his authority and face the enemy fearlessly.

What is authority?

Authority is delegated power.

Policemen who direct traffic during the rush hour just raise their hands and the cars stop. These men don't have the physical *power* to stop the vehicles if the drivers choose not to stop. But they don't use their own strength to stop traffic; they are strong in the *authority* that is invested in them by the government they serve. People recognize that authority and stop their cars. Blessed be God, there's authority that's vested in us by the Lord Jesus Christ!

Paul told believers to be strong in the Lord, and in the power of His might (Eph. 6:10). That means you can step out in front of the devil, hold up your hand, and tell him not to come any closer. Use your authority!

Once in England Smith Wigglesworth was standing on a street corner waiting for a bus. A woman came out of an apartment house, and a little dog ran out behind her. She said, "Honey, you're going to have to go back."

The dog didn't pay any attention to her. He just wagged his tail and rubbed up against her affectionately.

She said, "Now, dear, you can't go." The little dog wagged his tail and rubbed up against her again.

About that time, the bus arrived. The woman stomped her foot and yelled, "Get!" The dog tucked his tail between his legs and took off.

Wigglesworth said he hollered out loud without even thinking, "That's the way you've got to do with the devil!"

As a Roaring Lion

In 1942, while pastoring in East Texas, I had a test in my body. I didn't tell anyone about it except the Lord. I prayed and believed He would heal me. Then I stood my ground.

In the nighttime I would be awakened with alarming heart symptoms, and I would get up and pray. I battled that thing for about six weeks.

One night I had great difficulty in getting to sleep. Finally, after praying, I drifted off, and I had a dream. I am satisfied that God has spoken to me only four times in my life through dreams, but a dream like this one was no coincidence. It was from the Lord. When I woke up, I knew immediately what it meant. (If you don't know the meaning of a dream immediately, forget it.)

In this dream it seemed that another minister and I were walking on some kind of parade ground or ball field. There were stands on either side of us. As we were walking along talking, the man jumped and exclaimed, "Look!"

I turned and saw two ferocious, roaring lions. The man started running. I started running with him. Then I stopped and told him we were too far away from the stands to reach safety. We'd never escape those lions.

I stopped dead still, turned around, and went back to meet the lions. They came toward me with their fangs bared, roaring.

I was trembling. I told them, "I resist you in the Name of Jesus. In Jesus' Name you can't hurt me." I just stood there. They ran right up to me like a couple of kittens, sniffed around my ankles, and finally frolicked off, paying no attention to me.

Then I woke up. I knew exactly what God was saying to me. The Scripture in First Peter 5 came to me. It says, *"Be sober, be vigilant; because your adversary the devil, as a roaring lion, walketh about, seeking whom he may devour: Whom resist stedfast in the faith...."* (vv. 8,9).

The physical battle I had been fighting was won right then. Instantly the symptoms disappeared and I was all right. I had stood my ground. I wouldn't give in. I had won.

Ephesians 6:10 says, *"Finally, my brethren, be strong in the Lord, and in the power of his might."* Many people read that verse and think the Lord is telling them to be strong in themselves. But the Scripture doesn't say a word about being strong in yourself. It says to be strong in the Lord.

"I don't know whether I can make it or not," people say.

Certainly you can make it. Don't even think about it. Be strong in the Lord. Be strong in the power of *His* might, not your power or might.

First John 4:4 says, *"Ye are of God, little children, and have overcome them: because greater is he that is in you, than he that is in the world."*

"He that is in the world" is Satan, the god of this world and the head of principalities, powers, and rulers of the darkness of this world.

But the power that's in you is greater than the power that's in the world, because the power that backs our authority is greater than that which backs our enemies.

Prophecy

The Holy Spirit says, *"Power on earth invested in the Name of Jesus Christ and obtained by Him through His overcoming the enemy belongeth unto the Church. Therefore, exercise that authority, for it belongs to you on the earth, and in this life ye shall reign by Christ Jesus."*

Chapter 3
Seated With Christ

Matthew 28:18 is another verse where the word "authority" should have been used instead of "power." In the *King James Version* it reads, *"And Jesus came and spake unto them, saying, ALL POWER is given unto me in heaven and in earth."* It should read, "ALL AUTHORITY is given unto me in heaven and in earth."

When Christ ascended, He transferred His authority to the Church. He is the Head of the Church, and believers make up the Body. Christ's authority has to be perpetuated through His Body, which is on the earth. (Throughout Ephesians and elsewhere in the epistles, Paul uses the human body as an illustration of the Body of Christ.)

Christ is seated at the right hand of the Father — the place of authority — and we're seated with Him. If you know anything about history, you know that to sit at the right hand of the king or pope means authority. We died with Christ, and we were raised with Him. This is not something God is going to do in the future; He already has done it!

God's Mightiest Work

EPHESIANS 1:18-23
18 The eyes of your understanding being enlightened; that ye may know what is the hope of his calling, and what the riches of the glory of his inheritance in the saints,
19 And what is the exceeding greatness of his power to usward who believe, according to the working of his mighty power,
20 Which he wrought in Christ, when he raised him from the dead, and set him at his own right hand in the heavenly places,

11

> 21 Far above all principality, and power, and might, and
> dominion, and every name that is named, not only in this
> world, but also in that which is to come:
> 22 And hath put all things under his feet, and gave him
> to be the head over all things to the church,
> 23 Which is his body, the fulness of him that filleth all
> in all.

Notice especially the nineteenth verse: *"And what is the exceeding greatness of his power to usward who believe, according to the working of his mighty power."* In other words, there was such an overwhelming display of God's power in raising Jesus from the dead that *this actually was the mightiest work of God ever recorded!*

The Resurrection was opposed by Satan and all his cohorts. However, his forces were confused and defeated by our Lord Jesus Christ, who arose, ascended, and is now seated at the right hand of the Father, far above them.

Remember the text in Colossians 2:15? *"And having spoiled principalities and powers, he* [Christ] *made a shew of them openly, triumphing over them in it* [His death, burial, and resurrection]. *"*

These are the same demonic powers we have to deal with, but, thank God, Jesus defeated them. Other translations say He "put them to nought" or "paralyzed them."

In ancient times, victorious kings bringing back captives would have a parade, making a show of them openly. Jesus did this with the devil, putting him on display before three worlds — heaven, hell, and earth — after He defeated him. God gave us this account in the Scriptures so we in this world would know what had happened.

God wants us to know what happened in the death, burial, resurrection, and seating of Jesus Christ. He wants us to know that He has set Christ *"Far above all principality, and power, and might, and dominion, and every name that is named. . . ."* (Eph. 1:21).

The Source of Our Authority

The source of our authority is found in this resurrection and exalting of Christ by God. Notice in the eighteenth verse that the Holy Spirit through Paul prays that the eyes of the Ephesians' understanding — their spirits — might be opened to these truths. He wanted all churches — all believers — to be enlightened. The truth of the authority of the believer, however, is overlooked by many Christians. In fact, most churches don't even know the believer has any authority!

You never will understand the authority of the believer only with your intellect; you must get the spiritual revelation of it. You must believe it by faith.

EPHESIANS 2:1-7
1   And you hath he quickened, who were dead in trespasses and sins;
2   Wherein in time past ye walked according to the course of this world, according to the prince of the power of the air, the spirit that now worketh in the children of disobedience:
3   Among whom also we all had our conversation in times past in the lusts of our flesh, fulfilling the desires of the flesh and of the mind; and were by nature the children of wrath, even as others.
4   But God, who is rich in mercy, for his great love wherewith he loved us,
5   Even when we were dead in sins, hath quickened us together with Christ, (by grace ye are saved;)
6   And hath raised us up together, and made us sit to-

gether in heavenly places in Christ Jesus:
7 That in the ages to come he might shew the exceeding
riches of his grace in his kindness toward us through Christ
Jesus.

In the first verse we read, "*And you hath he quickened,
who were dead in trespasses and sins.*" Here the Holy
Spirit is saying through Paul, "According to the working
of the strength of His might *when He raised Him* from
the dead *and you* when you were dead."

You see, the same verb in Ephesians 1:20 that expresses the reviving of Christ from the dead expresses the
reviving of His people in Ephesians 2:1. In other words,
*the act of God that raised Christ from the dead also raised
His Body.* In the mind of God, when Jesus was raised from
the dead, we were raised from the dead!

Further into the second chapter we read, "*Even when
we were dead in sins,* [He] *hath quickened us together with
Christ, . . .And hath raised us up together, and made us
sit together in heavenly places in Christ Jesus*" (vv. 5,6).
This passage deals with the conferring of this authority.

Notice that the Head (Christ) and the Body (the
Church) were raised together. Furthermore, this authority
was conferred not only upon the Head, but also upon the
Body, because the Head and the Body are one. (When you
think of a person, you think of his head and body as one.)

As far as I know, churches believe that we were raised
up together with Christ. Why don't they believe that we've
been made to sit together with Him? If part of this verse
is so, the whole verse is so.

If the Church ever gets the revelation that we are the
Body of Christ, we'll rise up and do the works of Christ!
Until now, we've been doing them only limitedly.

When we realize that the authority that belongs to Christ also belongs to individual members of the Body of Christ and is available to us, our lives will be revolutionized!

1 CORINTHIANS 12:12-14,27
12 For as the body is one, and hath many members, and all the members of that one body, being many, are one body: so also is Christ. [We are Christ. He's calling the Body, which is the Church, Christ.]
13 For by one Spirit are we all baptized into one body, whether we be Jews or Gentiles, whether we be bond or free; and have been all made to drink into one Spirit.
14 For the body is not one member, but many . . .
27 Now ye are the body of Christ, and members in particular.

Thank God we are the Body of Christ!

2 CORINTHIANS 6:14,15
14 Be ye not unequally yoked together with unbelievers: for what fellowship hath righteousness with unrighteousness? and what communion hath light with darkness?
15 And what concord hath Christ with Belial? or what part hath he that believeth with an infidel?

The believer is called "righteousness," and the unbeliever is called "unrighteousness." The believer is called "light," and the unbeliever, "darkness." The believer is called "Christ," and the unbeliever, "Belial."

Seated With Christ

First Corinthians 6:17 says, *"But he that is joined unto the Lord is one spirit."* We are one with Christ. We are

Christ. We are seated at the right hand of the Majesty on High. All things have been put under our feet.

The trouble with us is that we've preached a "cross" religion, and we need to preach a "throne" religion. By that I mean that people have thought they were supposed to remain at the cross. Some have received the baptism in the Holy Spirit, have backed up to the cross, and have stayed there ever since.

We've sung "Near the cross, near the cross." Yes, we need to come by the cross for salvation, but we don't need to remain there; let's go on to Pentecost, the Ascension, and the throne!

The cross is actually a place of defeat, whereas the Resurrection is a place of triumph. When you preach the cross, you're preaching death, and you leave people in death. We died all right, but we're raised with Christ. We're seated with Him. Positionally, that's where we are right now: We're seated with Christ in the place of authority in heavenly places.

Many Christians know nothing about the authority of the believer. They really don't believe we have any authority. They believe they're barely saved and they must go through life being dominated by the devil while living on Barely-Get-Along Street. They magnify the devil more than they do God.

We need to be delivered from the bondage of death and walk in the newness of life. We're not at the cross. We died with Christ, but He has raised us up together with Him. Glory to God, learn how to take your place of authority.

The right hand of the throne of God is the center of power of the whole universe! Exercising the power of the throne was committed to the resurrected Lord.

We know that Christ with His resurrected physical body is there in full possession of His rights, awaiting the Father's time when His enemies shall be made His footstool. Hebrews 1:13 says, *"But to which of the angels said he at any time, Sit on my right hand, until I make thine enemies thy footstool?"*

The elevation of Christ's people with Him into the heavenlies clearly points to the fact that we are to sit with Him, sharing not only His throne but also His authority. That authority belongs to us!

No wonder Paul said, writing to the Romans, *"For if by one man's offence [spiritual] death reigned by one; much more they which receive abundance of grace and of the gift of righteousness shall reign in life by one, Jesus Christ"* (Rom. 5:17).

Several translations, including *The Amplified Bible*, say "reign as kings in life." Are we just going to reign when we get to heaven? No! We're to reign as kings *in life* by Jesus Christ. That's authority, isn't it? Whatever the king said was law; he was the last authority. We partake of the authority that Christ's throne represents.

Some of us have exercised a little more authority over the powers of the air than others because we have a little more spiritual comprehension, but God wants all of us to have that spiritual comprehension.

Maintaining Balance

The Holy Spirit prayed through Paul that we all might have wisdom, understanding, and authority over the demonic powers and the problems they create through their constant manipulation of men's minds.

It seems like it's the most difficult thing in the world for the Church to stay balanced. You can take any subject — including the authority of the believer — push it to the extreme, and it becomes harmful and ceases to bless. "Father Divine" was once saved and filled with the Holy Spirit. He had the real thing. Then he began studying these very Scriptures we have been studying. He reasoned, "If we are Christ, then I am Christ. Christ is God, so I am God." He founded a cult that was very popular. The people worshipped him.

It's easy to get into the ditch on either side of the road — into excess, wild fire, and fanaticism. Let's go down the middle of the road and maintain balance.

John Alexander Dowie, a Scotsman who received a revelation about divine healing while ministering before the turn of the century in Australia, crossed the ocean many times during his lifetime. He encountered many storms, but said every time a storm came up, he did what Jesus did: He rebuked the storm and it always ceased.

We should not be amazed by this, because Jesus said, "...*He that believeth on me, the works that I do shall he do also; and greater works than these shall he do; because I go unto my Father*" (John 14:12). Someone will ask what the "greater works" are. Well, let's just do the works Jesus did first and then think about the "greater works"!

Jesus didn't say that only a select few would do these works; He said those who believe on Him would.

As we study what the Word of God teaches and educate our spirits about the authority of the believer, I believe we'll be able to walk in this great truth more and more.

Chapter 4
Breaking the Power of the Devil

We see in Ephesians 6:12 that "...*we wrestle not against flesh and blood, but against principalities, against powers, against the rulers of the darkness of this world, against spiritual wickedness in high places*" [a marginal note calls them "wicked spirits in the heavenlies"].

The Word of God teaches us that these evil spirits are fallen angels who have been dethroned by the Lord Jesus Christ. Our contact with these demons should be with the knowledge that Jesus defeated them, spoiled them, put them to nought (Col. 2:15). And now that Jesus has dethroned them, we can reign over them!

Adam's Treason

Originally, God made the earth and the fullness thereof, giving Adam dominion over all the works of His hands. In other words, Adam was the god of this world. Adam committed high treason and sold out to Satan, and Satan, through Adam, became the god of this world. Adam didn't have the moral right to commit treason, but he had the legal right to do so.

Now Satan has a right to be here and be the god of this world until "Adam's lease" runs out. Satan had the right to rule over us until we became new creatures and got into the Body of Christ, as we see in Colossians 1: "*Giving thanks unto the Father... Who hath delivered us from the power of darkness, and hath translated us into the kingdom of his dear Son....*" (vv. 12,13).

That's why Satan has no right to rule us or dominate us. Yet the average Christian has more faith in Satan's

19

authority and power than in God's!

The Bible not only talks about the first man Adam, but also about the second Adam, Jesus Christ, who became our Substitute. In First Corinthians 15:45, He's called "the *last* Adam," and in the 47th verse He's called "the *second* man." All that Jesus did He did for us.

Our trouble is that we relegate everything to the future! Most church people believe we will exercise our spiritual authority sometime in the Millennium. If that is so, why does the Bible say Satan will be bound during the Millennium? There won't be any *need* to exercise authority then, because there will be nothing here that will hurt or destroy.

Authority Now

It's now, when there is something that will hurt and destroy, that we have authority. But many people believe we can't have much of anything now. They think Satan's running everything down here. We must remember, however, that although we are *in* the world, we are not *of* the world. Satan's running a lot of what is here on earth, but he's not running me. He's not running the Church. He's not dominating us. We can dominate him. We have authority over him!

Jesus said, *"Behold, I give unto you power to tread on serpents and scorpions, and over ALL the power of the enemy: and nothing* [nothing, nothing, nothing, nothing, nothing] *shall by any means hurt you"* (Luke 10:19).

Does the Church in this century have less authority than it did right after Jesus' death, burial, resurrection, ascension, and seating at the Father's right hand? If it has less authority today, it would have been better for

Jesus not to have died. But no, bless God, we *have* authority.

We need to build these truths into our lives by meditating and feeding upon them until they become a part of our consciousness. Naturally speaking, we eat certain foods every day because doctors tell us we need certain vitamins, minerals, etc., to build strong bodies. There are spiritual "vitamins" and "minerals," so to speak, we need to take every day, too, to be healthy Christians.

Jesus said in Matthew 28:18, "...*ALL POWER is given unto ME in heaven and in earth.*" All the authority that can be exercised upon the earth has to be exercised through the Church, because Christ is not here in person — in His physical body.

We are the Body of Christ. Even though we have prayed, "Now, Lord, You do this and that," leaving everything up to Him, He has conferred His authority on the earth to His Body, the Church. Thus, many problems exist because we *permit* them to — we're not doing anything about them. We're the ones who are supposed to do something about them, but we're trying to get someone else, including God, to do something about them.

This became real to me years ago when I was studying along this line. I couldn't explain it in my mind, but I knew it in my spirit. I began to understand this authority we have. While praying for my older brother's salvation, I heard the Lord, in my spirit, challenge me. He said, "*You do something about it!*"

I had been praying for my brother's salvation for many years. He was what you would call the "black sheep" of the family. In spite of my prayers, he seemed to get worse instead of better.

I always had prayed, "God save him." I'd even fasted.
I was prone to slip back into praying this way, but after
the Lord challenged *me* to do something about it — after
He told me I had the authority — I said, "In the Name
of Jesus, I break the power of the devil over my brother's
life, and I claim his salvation!"

I gave the order. I didn't keep saying it or praying it.
When a king gives an order, he knows it's going to be carried out.

The devil tried to tell me my brother never would be
saved, but I shut my mind off and started laughing. I said,
"I don't *think* he'll be saved — I *know* it! I took the Name
of Jesus and broke your power over him and claimed his
deliverance and salvation." I went my way whistling.
Within ten days, my brother was saved. The Word works!

How To Deal With the Devil

As long as Satan can keep you in unbelief or hold you
in the arena of reason, he'll whip you in every battle. But
if you'll hold him in the arena of faith and the Spirit, you'll
whip him every time. He won't argue with you about the
Name of Jesus — he's afraid of that Name.

I have found that the most effective way to pray can
be when you demand your rights. That's the way I pray:
"I demand my rights!"

Peter at the Gate Beautiful did not pray for the lame
man; he *demanded* that he be healed (Acts 3:6). You're not
demanding of God when you demand your rights; you're
demanding of the devil.

Jesus made this statement in John 14: *"And whatsoever ye shall ask in my name, that will I do ... If ye shall*

ask any thing in my name, I will do it" (vv. 13,14). He's not talking about prayer. The Greek word here is "demand," not "ask."

On the other hand, John 16:23,24 is talking about prayer: *"And in that day ye shall ask me nothing. Verily, verily, I say unto you, Whatsoever ye shall ask the Father in my name, he will give it you. Hitherto have ye asked nothing in my name: ask, and ye shall receive, that your joy may be full."* (The Father is mentioned here in connection with prayer, but He isn't mentioned in the passage from John 14.)

The Greek actually reads, "Whatever you *demand* as your rights and privileges . . . ." You've got to learn what your rights are.

Many years ago when I was pastoring a little church in Texas, a woman brought her violently insane sister to the parsonage to be prayed for. Because this woman had tried to kill herself and others, she had been in a padded cell for two years. However, her health had deteriorated, and doctors had recommended a furlough at home for her, because she was no longer considered dangerous.

When her sister introduced me as a "preacher," Scriptures started to roll out of this woman's mouth. She thought she had committed the unpardonable sin. The Lord told me to stand in front of her and say, "Come out, thou unclean devil, in the Name of Jesus!" I did that, but nothing happened. She just sat there looking like a statue.

I knew I had spoken the word of faith. You don't have to stand there all day long and command devils to come out. They're going to do it when you tell them to if you know your authority. They have to go once the command is given in faith.

Two days later I was told the woman was having a violent attack similar to the kind she had had when she first lost her mind. This news didn't disturb me. In the Bible we read that when Jesus rebuked the devil in such cases, people would fall and the devil would tear them. I knew the devil was just tearing this woman before he left her for good. I knew she wouldn't have any more spells, and she didn't. The doctors pronounced her normal and sent her home for good. Twenty years later she was happy and healthy, teaching a Sunday School class and working in a business.

Faith's Role in Authority

Faith is involved in exercising spiritual authority. Yes, there are times when evil spirits come out immediately, but if they don't when you speak the word of faith, don't get disturbed about it.

I base my faith on what the Word says. Some people's faith is not based on the Bible, however, it's based on a manifestation. They operate outside faith in the sense realm. If they get certain manifestations, they think the devil's gone. But he isn't gone just because you get a manifestation. He's still there, and you need to know that and exercise your authority.

When circumstances don't change immediately, some people become discouraged and slip back into the natural. They start talking unbelief and they defeat themselves. They give the devil dominion over them.

As Smith Wigglesworth often said, "I'm not moved by what I see. I'm not moved by what I feel. I'm moved only by what I believe." So stand your ground.

Before I received the baptism in the Holy Spirit, I was a young Baptist pastor. This was during the Depression, and I had a mother and a little brother to help support. My mother's small income paid the utilities, taxes, and insurance. My income bought our food.

I owned only one suit and an extra pair of pants. During those Depression days, much stealing went on, and someone stole both pairs of my pants. They were stolen on a Monday, and I was to preach that Thursday. So I prayed Tuesday as I left my job, "Lord, all I've got is a pair of khakis, and I can't preach in them. They are old work pants." I told the Lord that by Thursday I expected to see my stolen pants hanging right where they had been. I prayed that the person who had stolen them would be so miserable he would have to bring them back.

You see, it's a wrong spirit that makes someone steal. I was dealing with that *spirit* and not the person, because we have authority over spirits. I commanded the spirit to stop this action.

When I came home on Thursday afternoon, I knew those pants would be there, and they were there. So we can — and should — rise up against the devil.

Chapter 5
Exercising Authority

The door to exercising authority pivots upon two phrases Paul prayed for the Ephesians: "...*and set him at his own right hand in the heavenly places*" (Eph. 1:20), and "...*hath raised us up together*" (Eph. 2:6).

Meditate on these two prayers. Learn to pray them for yourself. Feed on their truths until they become a part of your inner consciousness. Then they will dominate your life. But don't try to accept them mentally; you've got to get the revelation of them in your spirit.

Notice that not only is Christ seated at the right hand of the Father, above all the powers in Satan's realm, but we're there, too, because God "*hath raised us up together.*" Not only have we been made to sit, but notice *where* we are sitting: "*Far above all principality, and power, and might, and dominion . . . .*" (Eph. 1:21).

In the mind of God, we were raised when Christ was raised. When Christ sat down, we sat down, too. That's where we are now, positionally speaking: We're seated at the right hand of the Father with Christ. (The act of Christ's being seated implies that, for the time being, at least, certain aspects of His work are suspended.)

All the authority that was given to Christ belongs to us through Him, and we may exercise it. We help Him by carrying out His work upon the earth. And one aspect of His work that the Word of God tells us to do is to conquer the devil! In fact, Christ can't do His work on the earth without us!

Someone will argue, "Well, He can get along without me, but I need Him."

No, He can't get along without you any more than you

can get along without Him. You see, *the truth that Paul is bringing out here in Ephesians is that Christ is the Head and we are the Body.*

What if your body said, "I can get along without the head. I don't need my head."

No, your body can't get along without your head. And what if your head said, "Well, I can get along without my body. I don't need it; I can get along without hands and feet." No, you can't.

Likewise, Christ can't get along without us, because the work of Christ and God is carried out through the Body of Christ. His work never will be done apart from us — and we never can get along without Him.

Ephesians 6:12 says, *"For we wrestle not against flesh and blood, but against principalities, against powers...."* If you take this verse out of its setting and go on talking about this awful fight we're in against the devil and describing how powerful the devil is, you've missed the whole point Paul was making — because that's not what he's saying in Ephesians.

Remember, when Paul wrote this letter to the Church at Ephesus, he didn't divide it into chapters and verses. Scholars did that at a much later date to help us in making reference. You can do great harm sometimes by picking one verse out of a chapter, taking it out of its setting, and making it say something it doesn't say.

The Holy Spirit through Paul already has said in the second chapter that we are seated *above* these powers that we have to deal with. Not only is Christ seated at the right hand of the Father, far above all these powers, but we're there, too, because God has made us sit together with Christ.

Therefore, in our battle against the enemy and his forces, we need to keep in mind that we're above them and we have authority over them. The Word tells us that Jesus has conquered them. Our job is to enforce His victory. His victory belongs to us, but we are to carry it out.

The Demon Jesus Refused To Deal With

In 1952, the Lord Jesus Christ appeared to me in a vision* and talked to me for about an hour and a half about the devil, demons, and demon possession.

At the end of that vision, an evil spirit that looked like a little monkey or elf ran between Jesus and me and spread something like a smoke screen or dark cloud.

Then this demon began jumping up and down, crying in a shrill voice, "Yakety-yak, yakety-yak, yakety-yak." I couldn't see Jesus or understand what He was saying.

(Through this entire experience, Jesus was teaching me something. And if you'll be attentive, you'll find the answer here to many things that have troubled you.)

I couldn't understand why Jesus allowed the demon to make such a racket. I wondered why Jesus didn't rebuke the demon so I could hear what He was saying. I waited a few moments, but Jesus didn't take any action against the demon. Jesus was still talking, but I couldn't understand a word He was saying — and I needed to, because He was giving instructions concerning the devil, demons, and how to exercise authority.

I thought to myself, *Doesn't the Lord know I'm not*

*See Rev. Kenneth E. Hagin's book *I Believe in Visions.*

*hearing what He wanted me to? I need to hear that. I'm
missing it!*

I almost panicked. I became so desperate I cried out,
"In the Name of Jesus, you foul spirit, I command you
to stop!"

The minute I said that, the little demon hit the floor
like a sack of salt, and the black cloud disappeared. The
demon lay there trembling, whimpering, and whining like
a whipped pup. He wouldn't look at me. "Not only shut
up, but get out of here in Jesus' Name!" I commanded.
He ran off.

The Lord knew exactly what was in my mind. I was
thinking, *Why didn't He do something about that? Why
did He permit it?* Jesus looked at me and said, "If you
hadn't done something about that, I couldn't have."

That came as a real shock to me — it astounded me.
I replied, "Lord, I know I didn't hear You right! You said
You *wouldn't,* didn't You?"

He replied, "No, if you hadn't done something about
that, I *couldn't* have."

I went through this four times with Him. He was em-
phatic about it, saying, "No, I didn't say I *would* not, I
said I *could* not."

I said, "Now, dear Lord, I just can't accept that. I never
heard or preached anything like that in my life!"

I told the Lord I didn't care how many times I saw Him
in visions — He would have to prove this to me by at least
three Scriptures out of the New Testament (because we're
not living under the Old Covenant, we're living under the
New). Jesus smiled sweetly and said He would give me
four.

I said, "I've read through the New Testament 150

times, and many portions of it more than that. If that is in there, I don't know it!"

Dealing With the Devil

Jesus replied, "Son, there is a lot in there you don't know."

He continued, "Not one single time in the New Testament is the Church ever told to pray that God the Father or Jesus would do anything against the devil. In fact, to do so is to waste your time. *The believer* is told to do something about the devil. The reason is because you have the authority to do it. The Church is not to pray to God the Father about the devil; the Church is to exercise the authority that belongs to it.

"The New Testament tells believers themselves to do something about the devil. The least member of the Body of Christ has just as much power over the devil as anyone else, and unless believers do something about the devil, nothing will be done in a lot of areas."

We believe that certain people have power. No, Jesus said *the least member of the Body of Christ has just as much power over the devil as anyone else;* and when we start believing that, that's when we're going to get the job done.

Jesus continued, "I've done all I'm going to do about the devil until the angel comes down from heaven, takes the chain and binds him, and puts him into the bottomless pit [Rev. 20:1-3]."

That came as a real shock to me.

"Now," He said, "I'll give you the four references that prove that. First of all, when I arose from the dead, I said,

'*All power* [authority] *is given unto me in heaven and in earth*' (Matt. 28:18). The word 'power' means 'authority.' But I immediately delegated my authority on earth to the Church, and I can work only *through* the Church, for I am the Head of the Church."

(Your head cannot exercise any authority anywhere except through your body.)

The second reference Jesus gave me was Mark 16:15-18:

> MARK 16:15-18
> 15 And he said unto them, Go ye into all the world, and preach the gospel to every creature.
> 16 He that believeth and is baptized shall be saved; but he that believeth not shall be damned.
> 17 And these signs shall follow them that believe; In my name shall they cast out devils; they shall speak with new tongues;
> 18 They shall take up serpents; and if they drink any deadly thing, it shall not hurt them; they shall lay hands on the sick, and they shall recover.

He said, "The very first sign mentioned as following *any believer* — not any pastor or any evangelist — is that they shall cast out devils. That means that in my Name they shall exercise authority over the devil, because I have delegated my authority over the devil to the Church."

Remember, Colossians 1:13 says, "*Who hath delivered us from the power of darkness, and hath translated us into the kingdom of his dear Son....*" (One translation says "*the Father* hath delivered us from the power of darkness.") Again that's the Greek word 'power' here for 'authority.'

The verse should read, "The Father hath delivered us

from the *authority* of darkness, and hath translated us into
the kingdom of his dear Son." God already has delivered
us from the authority of darkness! Therefore, we've got
a right to speak to darkness — that is, Satan and his
kingdom — and tell them what to do!

Exercising Authority Over Others

Believers have authority over the devil. They can break
the power of the devil if he raises his head anywhere in
their own life or the lives of their immediate family or loved
ones. They have authority there. They'll be free from the
enemy because they've got the right to exercise their
authority over him.

That doesn't mean, however, that they'll go down the
street casting the devil out of everyone they meet. It
primarily means they will exercise authority over the devil
in their own lives.

You've got to realize that you've got authority over
your own household that you don't have in my household.
Spiritual authority is much like natural authority. For
example, you don't have authority over my money. You
can't tell me what to do with my money unless I give you
permission to. You don't have authority over my children.

You can make the devil desist in some of his maneuvers
in somebody else's life, but you can't *always* cast him out,
because you don't have authority in that "household."
That's one place we've missed it.

The next reference Jesus gave me was James 4:7:
"...*Resist the devil, and he will flee from you*" (the
understood subject of this sentence is "you").

The believer has to have authority over the devil, or

the Bible wouldn't tell him to do something about the devil. This Scripture doesn't say that the devil will flee from Jesus; it says he'll flee from *you!*

Similarly, you don't pray that Jesus will lay hands on the sick; *you* do it. Notice, too, that the hands are not in the Head; the hands are in the Body: *"They . . . shall lay hands on the sick, and they shall recover."* When you lay hands on the sick, you are exercising authority over the devil.

That authority is yours whether you feel like you've got it or not. Authority has nothing to do with feelings. But you must exercise it.

After that vision, and after Jesus gave me that verse from James, my spirit told me the word "flee" was significant. I looked it up in the dictionary and found one of the shades of meanings was "to run from as if in terror." The devil will run from you in terror! Then I knew why the demon in my vision had begun to whimper and cry — he was terrified.

Since then I have seen other demons quake and quiver in fear as I exercised my God-given authority over them. They were not afraid of me, but of Jesus, whom I represent.

In the vision Jesus gave me another Scripture that tells us to do something about the devil. This third reference was from First Peter. Peter wrote, *"Be sober, be vigilant; because your adversary the devil, as a roaring lion, walketh about, seeking whom he may devour"* (1 Peter 5:8). Your adversary means your opponent.

This is as far as a lot of people read. They say, "Oh, the devil's after me!" They ask for prayer so the devil won't get them — but the devil's already got them if they talk that way. It's too late to pray then.

What are we going to do about him: Roll over and play dead? Hide our head in the sand and hope he'll disappear? No, thank God, notice what it says as we go on reading. The next verse reads, *"Whom resist stedfast in the faith, knowing that the same afflictions* [tests and trials] *are accomplished in your brethren that are in the world." The American Standard Version* says "your faith" instead of "the faith." I like that better.

Jesus said to me in this vision, "Peter did not write this letter and tell Christians, 'Now, word has come to me that God's using our beloved Brother Paul in casting out devils, and he's sending handkerchiefs or cloths, and the diseases are departing from people, and evil spirits are going out of them, so I would suggest that you write to Paul and get a handkerchief.' "

No, instead of that, he told *them* to do something about the devil. Why? Because they've got authority over him. The Spirit of God through the Apostle Peter wouldn't tell you to do something you couldn't do. The reason you can do it is because *every believer has the same authority Paul had in Jesus Christ.* Peter didn't tell us that only Paul could cast out devils or that Paul would resist the devil for us. (Why get Paul to do it when you can do it for yourself?)

Standing for Baby Christians

People are always asking me why they don't get healed. Some think there is something wrong with the preacher who prayed for them!

I explain that when they were first saved, they were

baby Christians, and God permitted others to pray for them and carry them on their faith. But after a while, God expects that baby to grow, walk, and start doing things for himself. God puts the baby down and tells him to walk, but many won't. Too many people still want to be babies and have someone else pray for them all the time.

We want to help those who can't help themselves, but we need to teach people so they can grow and use their own authority, because the time will come when they will have to use their own authority if they want their prayers answered.

Once my wife and I stayed in a certain couple's home while attending a convention. The woman had been in our church before she had married. They asked us to pray for their baby boy, just a few months old, who had a rupture. The doctors wanted to operate on him.

We cursed the rupture and commanded it to wither and die. In a matter of a few days, it had disappeared completely and the baby never had to have the operation.

The baby's mother said, "Brother Hagin, I don't mean to be critical, but in our church it seems that we younger people are the only ones who have any faith for healing. I didn't know who to ask to pray for the baby before you came, because no one ever gets healed here."

We ought to grow stronger in faith the older we get, but too often we don't. In her church, as in so many, most of the people were saved when they were younger, and God permitted others to pray for them then. But because of a lack of right teaching, they remained in that babyhood stage of Christian development. They said, "We used to get healed when we were first Christians, but now we don't."

It would make just as much sense for you never to have any clothes of your own — always depending on wearing somebody else's clothes — as it would for you never to exercise your own faith or do your own praying, always depending on somebody else's prayers.

What happens to people who never attempt to exercise any faith of their own, but always rely on other people's faith? We just read that "...*your adversary the devil, as a roaring lion, walketh about, seeking whom he may devour....*" But the believer can do something about him.

Jesus, James, and Peter tell us to do something about the devil. Paul says in Ephesians 4:27, "*Neither give place to the devil.*" This was the fourth Scripture Jesus gave me. He explained, "This means you are not to give the devil any place in you. He cannot take any place unless you give him permission to do so. And you would have to have authority over him or this wouldn't be true."

Authority on the Earth

Jesus added, "Here are your four witnesses. I am the first, James is the second, Peter is the third, and Paul is the fourth. This establishes the fact that the believer has authority on earth, for *I have delegated my authority over the devil to you on the earth.* If you don't do anything about it, nothing will be done. And that is why many times nothing *is* done."

Now you can understand why things have happened as they have. We've permitted them to happen! Not knowing our authority — not knowing what we could do — we have done nothing, and we actually have permitted the

devil to keep on doing whatever he wanted to do.
We need to realize this. Let's wake up. We may have
to change our way of praying and get after the devil. I
did. It won't hurt you to change; it's good for you. We
have authority to do this. We're sitting at the right hand
of the Father, far above principalities and powers. If we're
far above them, then we have authority over them.

Ephesians 1:22,23 goes on to say, *"And hath put all
things under his feet, and gave him to be the head over
all things to the church* [The feet are members of the body.
Feet aren't members of the head.], *Which is his body, the
fulness of him that filleth all in all."* As John A. MacMillan
pointed out, how wonderful to know that the least
members of the Body of Christ — those who are the very
soles of the feet, the little toenail, or the little toe — are
far above the mighty forces we have been considering.

Remember, Jesus said in Luke 10:19 to the other
seventy disciples that He sent out, *"Behold, I give unto
you power* [authority] *to tread on serpents and scorpions,
and over all the power of the enemy: and nothing shall by
any means hurt you."* How much authority over the devil
does the Church have? Any less than this? No, thank God,
no.

Yet if you'd listen to the average Christian talk or hear
some preachers preach, you'd get the impression that the
devil is bigger than everybody and that he's running
everything. Yes, he is the god of this world, so he's running the world system. But we're *in* this world, not *of* this
world, the Bible says, so he's not running us. The devil
has been walking on us too long.

These things are not joking matters. We're foolish to
make light jokes about these things. A preacher once said

to me at a convention, "Well, Brother Hagin, I've got the
devil on the run. The trouble is, I'm running and he's after
me!"

Making a statement like that just shows ignorance. In
the first place, you haven't any business running from the
devil. The Bible says he'll run from you. You need to put
him on the run. Unfortunately, I think that is the picture
of preachers and churches too much of the time; in fact,
most of the time. We see it everywhere.

Reigning as Kings

Let's look again at Romans 5:17, *"For if by one man's
offence death reigned by one; much more they which
receive abundance of grace and of the gift of righteousness
shall reign in life by one, Jesus Christ.)"* The Amplified
Bible says we shall "reign as kings in life through the One,
Jesus Christ, the Messiah, the Anointed One."

God's plan for us is that we rule and reign in life as
kings: to rule and reign over circumstances, poverty,
disease, and everything else that would hinder us. We reign
because we have authority. We reign by Jesus Christ. In
the next life? No, in *this* life.

If we're going to sing something or say something, let's
be sure it's in line with the Word of God. Some people sing,
"Here I wander, like a beggar, through the heat and the
cold," or "Precious Jesus, don't forget me" — all kinds
of unbelief.

We're not wandering like beggars, because we're not
beggars. We're children of God, heirs of God, joint-heirs
with Jesus Christ (Rom. 8:17). We're the Body of Christ.
We're seated with Christ at the right hand of Majesty on

High, far above all principalities and power and might and dominion, glory to God!

That doesn't sound like a beggar or "Precious Jesus don't forget me," or "If I can just make it in," or "Standing somewhere in the shadows you'll find Jesus," or "Lord, build me a cabin in the corner of gloryland."

I'd rather hear a donkey bray than listen to such songs, but we've sung them so long we believe they're true. People shed a few tears about "wandering like a beggar" and think they're getting blessed!

Too often we Christians act like young birds, having our eyes shut and our mouths wide open. Anybody can come along and feed us anything, and we're ready to accept it. Well, I'm not going to keep my mouth open and my eyes shut; I'm going to keep my eyes open and my mouth shut!

Humility vs. Poverty

For example, many Christians equate humility with poverty. One preacher once told me how humble another was because he drove a very old car. I replied, "That's not being humble — that's being *ignorant!*" Driving an old car was that preacher's idea of humility.

Another fellow remarked, "You know, Jesus and the disciples never drove a Cadillac!" There weren't any Cadillacs then. But Jesus did ride a donkey. It was the "Cadillac" of that day — the best means of transportation they had.

Believers have allowed the devil to cheat them out of every blessing they could enjoy. God didn't intend us to be poverty-stricken. He said we are to reign in life as kings.

Who would ever imagine a king being poverty-stricken?
The idea of poverty just doesn't go along with kings.

Exercising Authority in Your Family

God didn't intend for the devil to dominate our families.
When our children were small and the devil would try to
put sickness on them, I would get mad at the devil and
tell him to take his hands off my children. I would tell him,
"I'm ruling over my domain. You're not ruling in this
household; I am through Jesus Christ." I put him on the
run, and he ran. You can put him on the run, too.

Years ago I was preaching in the North, and I was
awakened in the middle of the night. Somehow I knew in
my spirit that somebody was in physical danger, and I
began to pray in tongues.

I asked the Lord what was wrong, and He showed me
it had to do with my older brother. I knew his life was in
danger. I continued praying quietly in tongues for about
an hour and a half. My praying didn't disturb my wife,
who was asleep in bed beside me. Finally I had a note of
victory, and I began to sing very quietly in other tongues.
Then I went back to sleep.

Two days later my sister called me from Texas. She
was crying and almost in hysterics. "Dub's been in an
accident, and he's broken his back," she cried. "He's in
terrible shape. He's in Kansas. The doctors don't know
whether he'll live or not."

"Wait a minute," I said. "Quiet down. He's not as bad
as they think. If he was, God's already touched him,
because I prayed about that two nights ago, and I've
already got the answer."

"Have you?"

"Yes, I have. Don't bother a bit about it. He's all right."

Two days later she called again. She had checked on his condition and had found that Dub had walked out of the hospital with his back in a cast. He hadn't died, like the doctors had predicted, and he wasn't paralyzed.

He came to our home in Garland, Texas, and was very despondent and depressed, because his wife had left him and had taken the children while he was gone. I was preaching in my home church that Sunday morning and I tried to get him to go with us, but he wouldn't. He was a baby Christian, just barely saved.

Right in the middle of my sermon, I suddenly had a vision. I had my eyes wide open, but out in front of me I saw my brother in the city park. I heard him say to himself, *Well, I know what I'm going to do. I'm going to kill her and then I'll kill myself.*

I stopped dead still and said, "Wait a minute. I've got a little matter I've got to take care of here. Then I'll get back to my sermon."

I spoke to that devil that was tormenting him: "Devil, you stop that right now! I adjure you in the Name of Jesus Christ to leave that man" (the congregation didn't know who I was talking about, but the devil did). That's all I said. Then I went back to my sermon.

When we got home, my brother was at the house, and he was obviously in good spirits. He said he had walked to the park and had decided to take matters into his own hands. I told him, "Well, I knew that," and I told him what I had seen.

He said, "Something came over me suddenly, and it

was like something lifted up from me. It was as if a cloud lifted from me, and I came back to the house whistling and singing."

Dub didn't know how to touch the Lord for himself because he was just a baby Christian. Sometimes those of us who are older in the Lord have to help baby Christians, and thank God we can. The time will come in their lives, however, when they will have to know how to do some things for themselves. We won't be able to act for them then.

Learn To Be Exalted

We Christians must learn that we are seated with Christ. We must learn to be exalted to the place where God wants us!

The Church fails too often in this ministry of authority. Instead, She is bowed down in defeat and is overcome with fear.

Ephesians 1:22 says, "*And hath put all things under his* [Jesus'] *feet, and gave him to be the head over all things to the church.*" Jesus is Head over sickness, disease, and anything else that's evil, as He proved when He was here on earth.

By reversing the words, we'll bring out the deepest meaning more clearly: "...head to the church over all things." Jesus is Head over all things for the Church's sake.

We need to meditate upon these divine truths so that our spirits may fully understand them. Once we do, we'll reap rich rewards. When we have this reverent attitude, the Spirit of truth, the Holy Spirit, can lift us into a place where we can see the true meaning of God's revelation. In Ephesians, Paul prayed that the Church at Ephesus also might have this spirit of wisdom and revelation.

God made Christ to be the Head over all things to the Church. It is for our sake that He's the Head, so that we through Him might exercise that authority over all things.

When we understand what belongs to us, we will enjoy the victory Christ has for us. The devil will fight to keep us from getting there, but through stubborn faith in Christ, the victory can be ours.

Chapter 6
Risen With Christ

In the Book of Colossians, Paul is writing to the Church at Colossae. Although he uses slightly different words, he says the same things he has said to the Ephesians about God's plan of redemption. He doesn't preach a new or different message to the Colossians.

COLOSSIANS 1:15-20
15 [Jesus] Who is the image of the invisible God, the firstborn of every creature:
16 For by him were all things created, that are in heaven, and that are in earth, visible and invisible, whether they be thrones, or dominions, or principalities, or powers: all things were created by him, and for him:
17 And he is before all things, and by him all things consist.
18 And he is the head of the body, the church: who is the beginning, the firstborn from the dead; that in all things he might have the preeminence.
19 For it pleased the Father that in him should all fulness dwell;
20 And, having made peace through the blood of his cross, by him to reconcile all things unto himself; by him, I say, whether they be things in earth, or things in heaven.

In the second chapter, we see that Christ was quickened by God the Father:

COLOSSIANS 2:12-15
12 Buried with him in baptism, wherein also ye are risen with him through the faith of the operation of God, who hath raised him from the dead.
13 And you, being dead in your sins and the uncircumcision of your flesh, hath he quickened together with him, having forgiven you all trespasses;
14 Blotting out the handwriting of ordinances that was against us, which was contrary to us, and took it out of

45

the way, nailing it to his cross;
15 And having spoiled principalities and powers, he made
a shew of them openly, triumphing over them in it.

Verse twelve says we were raised with Christ "through
the faith of the operation of God." Notice it was the Father
who did this work. Verse thirteen tells us that God not
only quickened us *at the same time* He quickened Christ,
but He also forgave our sins!

When Jesus the Righteous yielded to death, the bond
of the law against us was paid. The Father then blotted
out the broken laws and commandments which had stood
between Him and us. He nailed this cancelled bond to His
Son's cross.

Paul is saying here in Colossians that it was God who
formed the plan of redemption. It was God who raised
Jesus from the dead. It was God who gave Him a Name
above every other name. And it was God who spoiled the
demonic principalities and powers who opposed the resurrection of Christ.

Death is the penalty for sin. Therefore, when Christ
bore the world's guilt on the cross, the satanic powers of
the air sought to exercise their rights and hold Him under
their power.

The Keys of Authority

The Bible says Satan had the power of death — but
Jesus conquered him. Jesus says in Revelation 1:18, *"I am
he that liveth, and was dead; and, behold, I am alive for
evermore, Amen; and have the keys of hell and of death."*
Jesus Christ took the keys away from the devil, glory to
God! Keys belong to the Authorized One. Those are the

keys of authority.

We must remember that physical death is not of God; it is of the enemy. Death is still an enemy. The Bible says it is the last enemy that will be put underfoot. Thank God, that day's coming, but you don't have your new body yet. You'll meet people who believe they are going to live forever down here in the flesh, but notice none of them ever do. One fellow argued with me about this belief, and I replied, "If Paul never made it, you might as well forget it."

I can't understand how anybody could be that stupid and believe he's going to live forever in the flesh — in his present body. No, that body's got to be changed. You can't live forever in this present body. The Bible tells us when it will be changed: when Jesus comes. In a moment, in the twinkling of an eye, the bodies of us who are alive then will be changed and become immortal. Until then we have only a limited power over death.

After stripping the demonic powers of the authority that had been theirs, Christ *"made a shew of them openly, triumphing over them in it"* (Col. 2:15). Paul's statement here refers to the fact that Christ was elevated above His enemies to the right hand of the Father, a subject that Paul writes about in the Book of Ephesians, as we saw earlier. Again Paul is stressing the Father's work in the overthrow of satanic powers and the defeat of Satan himself.

In Ephesians we also saw that the Son is seated above these powers and has the authority of the throne of God. But this is precisely where the church world as a whole has failed. It has understood that Jesus Christ is the Supreme Head of the Church, but it has failed to understand that the Head is totally dependent on the Body for carrying out His plans; that we are seated with Christ in heavenly places; and that His exercising authority over the powers of the air has to be through the Body.

Now we can understand as never before what Jesus meant when He said, "...*Whatsoever ye shall bind on earth shall be bound in heaven: and whatsoever ye shall loose on earth shall be loosed in heaven*" (Matt. 18:18). That's using His authority upon the earth.

A few of us get a little glimpse of authority once in a while; some of us have sort of stumbled upon it and exercised it without realizing what we were doing. The thing that got me started studying along this line was when I asked myself the question: "Do we have authority that we don't know we have?"

When I began to study the subject, I found that we do have authority, thank God. I also found that heaven will back us up on what we refuse and what we allow. We've allowed a lot of things, but we just haven't exercised our authority. That's why things are as they are many times: We haven't done anything about the situation. We're waiting on God, and He's waiting on us, and He won't do anything until we act.

There have been times when I have been praying about a loved one near death, and the Lord has said to me, "I'll do whatever you tell Me to do." In one instance I asked the Lord to give the person two or three more years. He replied He would, just because I had asked Him to. He told me, "No earthly father desires to do more for his children than I do, if my children would just let Me!"

Some people think that God's a tyrant sitting on His throne holding a giant flyswatter in His hand. The minute you do something wrong, they believe He's ready to smash you to smithereens. But that's not a true picture of the Father.

The Lord is hindered in His plans because His Body has failed to appreciate the meaning of Christ's exaltation and the fact that we are seated with Him at the right hand of the Father. We have a part to play in this: We must cooperate with the Lord in faith.

Jesus said that the Holy Spirit, who comes to dwell in us when we are born again, would guide us into all truth. A preacher once picked up a Bible and threw it to the floor, declaring he didn't need it because he had the Holy Spirit. But he did need the Bible, because you can't follow the Holy Spirit into truth apart from the Bible.

When you get out beyond the written Word of God, you're getting out too far. Stay with the Word.

The Word of God is from the Spirit of God: Holy men of old wrote it. The Word of God is of utmost importance. But you'll never understand it with your head; you must understand it with your heart.

Don't put the Spirit above the Word. Put the Word first and the Spirit second, and you'll be safe.

The well-known Pentecostal editor Stanley Frodsham, the author of Smith Wigglesworth's biography, brought out the fact that Wigglesworth was, first of all, a man of God's Word, and, second, a man filled with the Spirit of God. That's an excellent combination.

Chapter 7
The Armor of God

The believer must continually be arrayed with spiritual armor. Ephesians 6:10,11 says, *"Finally, my brethren, be strong in the Lord, and in the power of his might. Put on the whole armour of God, that ye may be able to stand against the wiles of the devil."*

The Christian who puts on this armor and engages in spiritual warfare is marked. By spiritual warfare I simply mean doing the works of Jesus and taking our authority over the devil as we go about our daily lives. I am not talking about purposely trying to go head-to-head with Satan in some kind of prayer combat. The devil will do everything in his power to keep you from coming into this knowledge of authority over him. He'll fight you more over this than any other subject. Then, after you have come to the knowledge of this authority, he'll oppose you and try to steal it from you. There will be tests, and sometimes people fail those tests. The devil wants you to throw up your hands and say the authority of the believer won't work for you.

A man once came to me in a meeting where I was preaching on this and said the authority of the believer wouldn't work for him. I told him if it doesn't work, God is a liar. (This man was, in essence, calling God a liar.)

I'd rather die than say God's Word doesn't work. If it doesn't work, it's because *I* don't work it. We may fail, but God's Word doesn't fail. I believe His Word is true.

The enemy will resist your interference in his sphere, because he's exercising authority over the powers of the air, and he wants to continue to do so. When you interfere with Satan's kingdom by exercising your spiritual authority, he will attack you in an attempt to get you to back down from using that authority.

If you successfully resist Satan's attacks in one area, he will come against you in another area. You may as well get ready for these attacks, because they're coming. In other words, your privileged spiritual position makes you an enemy to the devil.

You see, the devil realizes he cannot hold in bondage a believer who knows his authority in Christ Jesus. Such a believer is aware that he is seated with Christ in heavenly places and that the devil is a defeated foe under his feet (Eph. 1:15-2:6). Furthermore, this believer is convinced that no work of the enemy can prevail against him in carrying out the will of God on the earth.

How To Remain Undefeated

If believers take advantage of the spiritual armor provided for them, the enemy cannot defeat them. I don't believe that anything that's of the enemy should be able to defeat those of us who are members of the Body of Christ.

The believer *must* continually be arrayed with this armor. The Holy Spirit prayed through Paul that the eyes of the people would be opened to know this full provision that has been made for their safety. Spiritual armor is outlined in Ephesians 6:

EPHESIANS 6:10-17
10 Finally, my brethren, be strong in the Lord, and in the power of his might [not your might].
11 Put on the whole armour of God, that ye may be able to stand against the wiles of the devil.

12 For we wrestle not against flesh and blood, but against principalities, against powers, against the rulers of the darkness of this world, against spiritual wickedness [or wicked spirits] in high places.
13 Wherefore take unto you the whole armour of God, that ye may be able to withstand in the evil day, and having done all, to stand. [If you put on the whole armor of God, you'll stand.]
14 Stand therefore, having your loins girt about with truth, and having on the breastplate of righteousness;
15 And your feet shod with the preparation of the gospel of peace;
16 ABOVE ALL, taking the shield of faith, wherewith ye shall be able to quench all the fiery darts of the wicked. [Not one fiery dart should get through to your body, soul, or mind, because you've got the shield of faith.]
17 And take the helmet of salvation, and the sword of the Spirit, which is the word of God.

The different parts of this armor symbolize spiritual truths which belong to the believer. Wearing this armor, the believer is protected and unhampered in his ministry of authority. All he needs to be concerned about is keeping his armor bright and well secured about him. Now let's take a closer look at this armor:

First, as John A. MacMillan taught, there's the girdle of *truth*, which represents a clear understanding of God's Word. Like a soldier's belt, it holds the rest of the armor in place.

Second is the breastplate of *righteousness*. This has a twofold application: Jesus is our Righteousness, and we put Him on first. It also shows our obedience to the Word of God.

Third, our feet are shod with the preparation of the Gospel of *peace*. This is a faithful ministry proclaiming the Word of God.

Fourth is the shield of *faith.* A shield is a covering for the entire body. This represents our complete safety under the blood of Christ, where no power of the enemy can penetrate.

Fifth is the helmet of *salvation,* referred to in First Thessalonians 5:8 as the hope of salvation. The hope of salvation is the only helmet able to protect the head in these days of turning from the truth.

Sixth is the sword of the Spirit, which is *the Word of God.* This shows that the Word of God is to be used offensively. The other parts of the armor are mainly defensive, but the sword — the Word of God — is an active weapon. Dressed in the armor of God, you are prepared to withstand every attack of the enemy.

Chapter 8
Authority Over Demon Spirits, Not Human Wills

Although we have authority over demon spirits, we do not have authority over our fellowmen or their wills. We miss it a lot of times in thinking that we do.

We have authority over demons, and we can control them as far as our lives or our family's lives are concerned, but we can't always control them when other people are concerned, because that person's will comes into play.

Many years ago I was holding a meeting here in Oklahoma, and as I was ministering to the sick in the healing line, I had an inward intuition — I knew by the inward witness — that somebody in the line had a demon in him. That doesn't mean he was demon possessed — that's a different thing entirely. To be possessed is to be taken over entirely — spirit, soul, and body. You can *have* a demon in your body without being *possessed* by a demon.

I kept looking around. When a certain man stood within four persons of me, I knew the demon was in him. I never said anything out loud.

You have to realize this: Although the devil does know some things, he is not all-knowing, or omniscient, like God is. Because of his psychic powers, you can see that the devil does know some things. Some fortunetellers do predict events that come to pass. *The devil even knows some of your thoughts.* How do we know this? Because mind readers often can read your mind and tell you what you're thinking. And they don't do that by the power of God.

Before the man stepped in front of me I thought to

myself, *I'm going to cast that thing out of him.* I didn't
say anything out loud; I just thought it. When he stepped
up in place, before I could say anything, he spoke up. The
demon spoke through him, whining in a high-pitched, nasal
voice, "You can't cast me out! You can't cast me out! You
can't cast me out!"

I said, "Yes I can, in the Name of Jesus."

He said, "No you can't. This man wants me to stay.
And if he wants me to stay, I can."

I said, "You're right," and passed him by.

Religious Spirits

Several days later I saw that man on the street,
stopped him, and engaged him in conversation. He wasn't
crazy; he had all his mental faculties. As I talked to him,
I found out what kind of a spirit he had. It was a religious
spirit. People need to know there are such spirits. They
make people act very religious. Actually, this fellow had
three evil spirits in him. The others were deceiving and
lying spirits.

He believed in a mixture of some Bible along with
eastern religions. He leaned more toward the eastern
religions. I talked to him about this. I said, "Those
beliefs are not scriptural. They're not according to the New
Testament."

He replied, "Bible or no Bible, I like it this way, and
I'm going to stay with it."

I said, "Anytime you want to get rid of those devils,
come to see me. But as long as you want it that way, that's
the way it's going to be."

He said, "Well, that's the way I want it."

Free Will Prevails

You've got to walk off and leave people when they want it that way. If people want to live in sin, they can. If they want to be free, they can be free. But as long as they don't want to be free, neither Jesus nor anybody else can set them free.

You can't go around promiscuously exercising authority over the devil in somebody else. You've got authority over your own life and with your own family. But you can't cast the devil out of everyone you meet on the street, even if they *do* have the devil in them, because they have authority over their own lives. When people want help, that's another matter.

It's strange that sometimes even Spirit-filled people don't want help. In 1954 I preached for the first time in the state of Oregon. I started off on Sunday night preaching an evangelistic type of sermon. On Monday night I preached on faith. I announced that there would be a healing service Tuesday night.

In those days, I'd put people in the same line, whether they came for salvation, the baptism in the Holy Spirit, or healing. I ministered to them one at a time.

I came to a woman. There was a man with her, and he did all the talking. She never said anything. I could tell by looking at her that she wasn't right mentally. The man said his wife was very nervous and had spent some time in a mental institution.

Let me point something out to you here. You don't just exercise spiritual authority on behalf of other people per se; you've got to have the manifestation of the Spirit of God. That's why many are failing. They are trying to deal with spirits without the word of knowledge, discerning of spirits, or any unction of the Holy Ghost.

When Jesus once talked to me about the devil, demons, and demon possession,* He used as an example the girl possessed with a spirit of divination. She followed Paul and Silas around Philippi *"for many days,"* according to Acts 16:18, saying, "*...These men are the servants of the most high God...."* (v. 17).

Jesus asked me this question: "Do you know why Paul didn't deal with that spirit the first day?"

I said, "No, I really don't. I've wondered about it. Why didn't Paul, an apostle, a man of God, a man of authority, just take authority over that evil spirit the first day?"

Jesus said, "He had to wait for the manifestation of the Spirit; he had to wait until the Spirit of God gave him discerning of spirits."

You see, you can run the devil away from you or your house anytime. If a person is on your premises, you also have authority over him. But when you get away from where *your* domain is, the evil spirits have a right to be there, because Satan is the god of this world!

That's the reason Paul had to wait many days to deliver the demon-possessed girl. He didn't command that spirit to leave her the first day she began following him. He waited, and when the right time came, he spoke to that spirit, and it came out of her.

When I laid hands on the woman in the healing line, I didn't see any spirits, but I had a word of knowledge. I didn't have discerning of spirits operating in my ministry

---

*For an account of Rev. Kenneth E. Hagin's major visions of Jesus, *see* his book, *I Believe in Visions.*

then but I had the word of knowledge operating. When I laid hands on her, her life ran off in front of me as if I were seeing it on a television screen, and I knew the whole story.

I said to her husband, "I'm not going to minister to her. Take her to the pastor's study. When the meeting's over, I'll bring the pastor with me and I'll talk to both of you." So he took her away.

The pastor and I went to his study. I found out that the woman's husband was a deacon in this church. I told him, "I wanted the pastor here as a witness. He'll tell you he hasn't said one word to me about your wife. I don't know anybody in this state but this pastor. I never saw you or your wife before.

"I'll tell you why I did not minister to your wife in public. When I laid my hands on her, I knew on the inside of me — I could see it all in an instant — that your wife once heard an evangelist say the Lord had spoken to him in an audible voice. She began to seek that God would speak to her in an audible voice, too.

"What she failed to realize was that the evangelist didn't say he was *seeking* for God to speak to him that way — he didn't ask God to do it — he was just waiting on God. (When you begin seeking an audible voice, the devil will accommodate you. It's wrong to do this.)

"Demons began to speak to her," I continued. "She began to hear these voices, and they drove her crazy. You told me she had been in an institution once. Actually she has been there twice, hasn't she?"

The husband replied, "Who told you?"

"The Lord," I said. "He also showed me that you took your wife to a healing meeting, and the evangelist couldn't get her delivered, so you're mad at him. Then I saw in the Spirit that you took her to a prophet's meeting, and he couldn't get her delivered, and now you're mad at him. I wouldn't be able to get her delivered any more than the two of them, and you'd be mad at me. And that's the reason I wouldn't minister to her.

"Now I'm going to tell you why they didn't deliver her and why I can't deliver her: *She doesn't want to be delivered.* As long as she wants to hear these voices, she's going to hear them. She's not crazy. She's hearing everything I'm saying."

I turned to her and said, "Now, Sister, when you get to the place where you don't want to hear these voices, you come and I'll help you."

"Well," she said, "I want to hear these voices."

I said, "I know you do."

Someone may say, "Well, maybe she didn't know what she was talking about." If she hadn't known, the Lord would have told me. I'd have known that, too.

The Bible says, concerning the ministry of Jesus, that He cast spirits out with His Word. It also says that He cast them out by the Spirit of God. It wasn't just His Word speaking apart from the Spirit of God. Read the twelfth chapter of Matthew. The Pharisees were accusing Jesus of casting out demons by Beelzebub, the prince of the devils (v. 24).

Jesus replied, "*. . .if I cast out devils by the Spirit of God, then the kingdom of God is come unto you*" (v. 28).

We know from the Word that we have spiritual authority, but we must depend upon the Holy Spirit to help us in ministering authority. We can't do it by ourselves.

As I mentioned earlier, if the devil attacks me, I have

authority over him, because I have authority over my own life. I can tell him to leave my house immediately. I also can control situations as long as people are in my presence.

For example, a pastor friend of mine from Fort Worth, Texas, once accompanied me to a campmeeting I was to preach in California. He had suffered from sugar diabetes for many years and had to test his urine every morning to determine how much insulin he needed for his daily injection.

Trying to teach him a lesson of faith, I turned to him as we pulled out of the driveway of his parsonage and I said, "You'll never register any sugar as long as you're with me."

You see, I could control that disease as long as he was with me — as long as he was on my premises. But I couldn't control it when he was away from me. I would have to train him to exercise spiritual authority for himself.

He looked at me as if he didn't believe me, but he was with me almost two weeks and he never registered any sugar, even though he ate pie and cake.

"Now I know I'll register sugar today," he would say. After testing himself, he'd say, "That beats anything I've ever seen in my life!" He later told me he was home three days before he started registering sugar again.

You see, I had claimed authority over that disease. Although I had control over the unseen force, I didn't have control over the pastor's will. I could control the unseen force as long as the pastor was in my presence, and I tried to convince him that he could exercise the same authority, but he didn't catch on. He *expected* the diabetes to return, and it did. It took him five years before he finally understood spiritual authority. (Some of us preachers are slow!) If I could have been with other people constantly, I could have helped them, too, but I can't live with people; I don't have time.

Breaking the Devil's Power

Years ago when my older brother was bound by the devil, I said, "Satan, in the Name of Jesus Christ, *I break your power over my brother's life,* and I claim his deliverance and salvation!" In approximately two weeks he was saved. I had been trying to get him saved for 15 years, but nothing had ever worked. When I took this stand and exercised my spiritual authority as a believer, it worked.

Someone heard me say this and said they would try it and see if it worked. I knew it wouldn't work for them, because I hadn't *tried* it — I had *done* it.

Sometimes believers say they will try something because it has worked for someone else. If they study God's Word and clothe themselves in its teaching on authority, it will work for them. But if they try to act on God's Word without really having that Word built up in their spirit, the devil will defeat them soundly.

You'll only defeat the devil when you've got a foundation of God's Word and you act upon it. The Bible says (speaking of Satan), *"Whom resist stedfast in the faith..."* (1 Peter 5:9). Your level of faith is directly related to the degree of God's Word dwelling in your heart, that is, that Word which is reality to you and in which you are daily walking.

Why People Lose Their Healing

When people are in a place where faith is high — where there's a mass faith — or where the gifts of the Spirit are in operation, it's comparatively easy for them to receive healing. This is what happens in big meetings — I saw it happen in the well-known evangelists' meetings during the days of the Healing Revival, which was from 1947-58.

However, when these people get back on their own, the devil comes along with lying symptoms. The people don't have a foundation of faith in them, and the devil puts the same thing back on them. That's the reason you see people get delivered from evil spirits, sickness — a lot of things — and the next time you see them, they're right back where they were.

Somebody will say, "Well, they never got healed to begin with."

How could a crippled man walk who had never walked before if he hadn't been healed? If that wasn't healing, what was it? How could a blind man see — I've seen them do it — who had never seen before? How could a deaf person hear who had never heard before?

They were all right until they got home, and after two or three weeks, their healing was gone. Why did they lose it? Because they didn't know their authority. They didn't know how to hold onto what they had, so they didn't try to exercise authority themselves; or, if they said anything, they said the wrong thing.

I've seen polio victims completely healed — their feet and legs straightened out — and in 10 days' time they lost their healing.

I remember one woman who had been completely bed-

fast with arthritis for three years. She was stretched out
stiff as a board in her bed. She was healed instantly, got
up, and walked. Her doctor couldn't find a trace of arthritis
in her body. But six weeks later she was as stiff as a board
again. Why did she lose her healing?

Some people say, "They hypnotize them." Is that it?
No, people get into the presence of God where the gifts
of the Holy Spirit are in operation and it's easy to receive
healing. Then, when they get back on their own, they're
really on their own.

That's why people need to be taught the Word of God
and their rights and privileges as believers. Then they can
exercise authority for themselves over the devil, diseases,
and circumstances.

Casting Out Demons

The Bible differentiates between casting out devils and
healing the sick. Often people's physical conditions don't
respond to prayer and the laying on of hands because there
is an evil spirit involved.

This happened in the case of a Baptist woman in New
Orleans. She was mentally deranged and confined to an
institution. One day a friend of mine, a Baptist minister
who had received the baptism in the Holy Spirit, went to
pray for her. He cast seven devils out of her, and immediately she was well.

A university professor who was acquainted with her
case used it as an illustration in his lectures. It made such
an impression on him that he invited the Baptist minister
to discuss it with him. As a result, the professor's wife
received the baptism in the Holy Spirit. The professor not

only sought to be filled, but he incorporated into his teachings the fact that demons have more effect on people than was thought.

Oppression vs. Possession

Back in the 1950s a church member came in my healing line, and I realized the man had a demon in his body. This man had been in nearly every well-known evangelist's healing line, but he hadn't gotten healed, because that spirit that was oppressing him had to be dealt with. This wasn't a case for healing.

In praying for him, I explained to the people, "This man's body is *oppressed* by a demon. He is not *possessed* by a demon. I'll use this illustration: Suppose you live in a house built nearly one hundred years ago, and somebody tells you, 'That house has got termites in it.' That doesn't mean you've got termites in *you!*

"Your body is the house you live in. If you know how, you can keep the termites out of your natural house — and the demons out of your physical house. They won't be there if you use the right precautions."

I once heard a Spirit-filled psychiatrist who donated time to charity hospitals in his area. In one mental institution he decided to experiment with a man who hadn't spoken in three years. The man stared straight ahead with no expression, like a statue.

The doctor said, "I laid hands on him every day and said, 'If there are evil spirits here, I rebuke them and command every one of them to leave in the Name of the Lord Jesus Christ.' "

If the other doctors weren't around, this doctor would

lay hands on the patient and pray out loud over him five minutes a day in tongues. If the other doctors were around, he used wisdom, knowing they wouldn't be able to understand what he was doing, and he'd pray silently.

In 10 days' time the patient was talking, and in 30 days he was sent home as cured. The doctor helped other patients as well. God honors faith, and the Spirit of God knows how to pray. He's the Author of prayer.

How To Deal With Demons

We've got to depend on the Spirit of God to know when demons are present and to know how to deal with them. We're helpless without both the Spirit and the Word. Don't just be a Word person without the Spirit, and don't just be a Spirit person without the Word. Many try to act on the Word of God without the Spirit of God. You've got to have both of them. The Spirit and the Word agree.

You don't need to deal with a spirit in every case of healing. But if you have to, the Lord will show you. The way I see it, God's an intelligent Being, and I'm an intelligent being, and He can tell me if an evil spirit is present. *I go as much by what He doesn't say as I do by what He does say.* If He doesn't say anything, I don't try to deal with an evil spirit. I go on and minister healing to the person.

What is strange is that I'll be led to minister healing in one instance and then in seemingly an identical case I'll have to deal with a spirit. I don't understand it, but I know from experience it works that way. You can't judge one case by another.

Helpless people need to be helped. Sometimes you can

carry them on your own faith. But people who know — people who are enlightened — have to walk in the light of what they know. Some people are more enlightened than others. The more you know, the more is required of you.

You can be released from oppression to your body and your mind. You can exercise spiritual authority over others as long as they are in your presence. You can take authority over all unseen forces.

If you learn how to exercise spiritual authority like this, it will work in your home as well. I've heard of women who exercised their spiritual authority when their unsaved husbands came home arguing and fighting. The women had learned how to quietly and calmly rebuke the evil spirits behind the situation and claim authority over them — and the situation changed.

I learned how to do this years ago when some of my relatives would get extremely angry. I simply took authority over the situation. They knew when I did it, because they looked at me with a startled expression — and they straightened out immediately. I wasn't exercising authority over their *will*, however, but over the *spirit* that made them act the way they did.

Jesus once told His disciples that He was going to Jerusalem to suffer many things and to die. Peter objected. Jesus immediately rebuked him, saying, *"Get thee behind me, Satan...."* (Matt. 16:23).

Jesus wasn't saying that Peter was Satan. He was showing that Peter had sided in with doubt, unbelief, and the devil. Sometimes Christians unconsciously yield to the enemy, but we can take authority over that spirit.

The Bible says that we also can take authority over fear — even fear in our own lives. We need to know that.

However, we can't always take authority over fear in somebody else's life. I've been able to control fear as long as a person was in my presence and didn't know how to stand against it.

Second Timothy 1:7 says, *"For God hath not given us the spirit of fear; but of power, and of love, and of a sound mind."* Notice that the Bible calls fear a spirit. God has given us a spirit of power, love, and a sound mind.

Even when I was a young Baptist pastor, I always took authority over fear and doubt. If I was tempted to doubt, I would say, "Doubt, I resist you in the Name of Jesus." If I was tempted to fear, I would say, "Fear, I resist you in the Name of Jesus." Doubt and fear will leave you when you do this.

We even have authority over those who oppose the truth.

In Texas there was a Full Gospel minister who lived next door to a policeman. The policeman belonged to a denomination that is vehemently opposed to speaking in tongues.

The minister got the policeman to visit his church. Then the policeman somewhat jokingly asked the minister to go with him to his church. The minister decided to go because the policeman told him his minister was going to speak on the subject of tongues.

During his sermon, this minister didn't base any of his remarks on the Bible, but told about different things he'd heard had happened among these "tongue talkers." Then he began imitating speaking in tongues. Hearing this, the Full Gospel minister took authority over the situation. The speaker stopped abruptly, turned pale, and sat down without finishing his sermon.

The policeman realized what had happened. Afterwards he went to the Full Gospel pastor, shook his hand, and hugged him. He said, "Bless God, I'm glad God arrested him. He ought to have had more sense than that."

The next night the preacher apologized for talking about something he didn't know much about. He said he felt as if God had arrested him, and he added that it is better to leave things alone when we don't know much about them.

Resist the Devil

Often we realize that certain trials in our lives are the work of the enemy, and we cry out to God to rebuke him and alter circumstances for us. However, God's Word tells us to rebuke the enemy ourselves. In James 4:7 we are told, *"Resist the devil, and he will flee from you."* The authority over the devil is ours. The responsibility is ours.

If we'll resist the devil, he will flee from us. The Bible doesn't say, "Get somebody else to resist the devil for you"; it says *we* are to resist the devil. Too many of us sit idly by, waiting for Jesus to do something when *we* are the ones who are supposed to resist the devil. Why? Because we have the authority to! (We always want somebody else to do what we're supposed to do.)

Of course we're always going to have spiritual babies, and we ought to carry them on our faith, but some of us ought to grow up enough to be able to help look after the babies and not leave it up to the pastor to do everything.

Conditions exist because we permit them to. Matthew 18:18 says, *"Verily I say unto you, Whatsoever ye shall bind on earth shall be bound in heaven: and whatsoever*

ye shall loose on earth shall be loosed in heaven."
That was the *King James Version.* I like another translation I once read which renders it, "Whatsoever things ye refuse to be permitted on earth will be refused to be permitted in heaven."
Exercise your authority!